from SEA TO SHINING SEA

MASSACHUSETTS

By Dennis Brindell Fradin

CONSULTANTS

Donald A. Doliber, M.A., Author and Social Studies Teacher,
Masconomet Regional School District, Boxford, Massachusetts

Robert L. Hillerich, Ph.D., Consultant, Pinellas County Schools, Florida;
Visiting Professor, University of South Florida

CHILDRENS PRESS®
CHICAGO

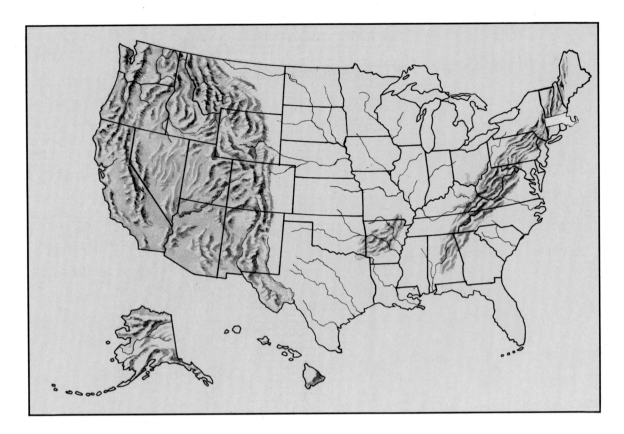

Massachusetts is one of the six states in the region called New England. The other New England states are Connecticut, Maine, New Hampshire, Rhode Island, and Vermont.

For my niece, Lauren Bloom, who is beautiful, intelligent, and a great cranberry counter

Front cover picture: The North Bridge, Concord; page 1: a view of the Boston skyline from the Back Bay; back cover: Boston at dusk

Project Editor: Joan Downing
Design Director: Karen Kohn
Research Assistant: Judith Bloom Fradin
Typesetting: Graphic Connections, Inc.
Engraving: Liberty Photoengraving

Library of Congress Cataloging-in-Publication Data

Fradin, Dennis B.
　From sea to shining sea. Massachusetts / by Dennis
Brindell Fradin.
　　p. cm.
　Includes index.
　Summary: An introduction to the history, geography,
important people, and interesting sites of Massachusetts.
　　ISBN 0-516-03821-4
　1. Massachusetts—Juvenile literature.
　[1. Massachusetts.] I. Title.
F64.3.F66　1991　　　　　　　　　　　　　91-541
974.4–dc20　　　　　　　　　　　　　　　　CIP
　　　　　　　　　　　　　　　　　　　　　AC

Faneuil Hall, Boston

Table of Contents

Introducing the Bay State

Massachusetts is located in the northeastern United States. Few states are smaller. Yet Massachusetts is a giant in one way. It was the scene of more famous events in the 1600s and 1700s than any other part of America.

Massachusetts' first colonists were the Pilgrims from England. The Pilgrims sailed to Massachusetts on the *Mayflower* in 1620. The next year, the Pilgrims began Thanksgiving in America. A few years later, other English people called Puritans arrived. The Puritans founded Boston, the capital of Massachusetts. They founded America's first public school. The Puritans also built America's first college—Harvard—near Boston.

England ruled thirteen American colonies, including Massachusetts, for many years. Then, in 1765, the thirteen colonies began to rebel. Massachusetts led the fight against England. The Boston Tea Party helped bring on war. When the

*A picture map
of Massachusetts*

Revolutionary War
began in 1775, the
first shots were fired
in Massachusetts.

The Bay State has
many other claims to fame.
Where did Paul Revere make
his famous ride? What state produced
a father and son who both were
president? Where was women's-rights champion
Susan B. Anthony born? Where do the Red Sox play
baseball and the Celtics play basketball? The answer
to these questions is the little state with the big
name: Massachusetts!

*Overleaf: Annisquam
Harbor Lighthouse,
Cape Ann*

5

Ocean on the East,
Mountains on the West

OCEAN ON THE EAST, MOUNTAINS ON THE WEST

The northeastern corner of the United States is called New England. English people of the 1600s coined the name. They thought the region looked like England. The New England states are Massachusetts, Connecticut, Maine, New Hampshire, Rhode Island, and Vermont. All six are small. In fact, only five states in the nation are smaller than Massachusetts.

Every other New England state but Maine borders Massachusetts. Vermont and New Hampshire are to the north. Rhode Island and Connecticut are

Massachusetts could fit inside the largest state, Alaska, about seventy times!

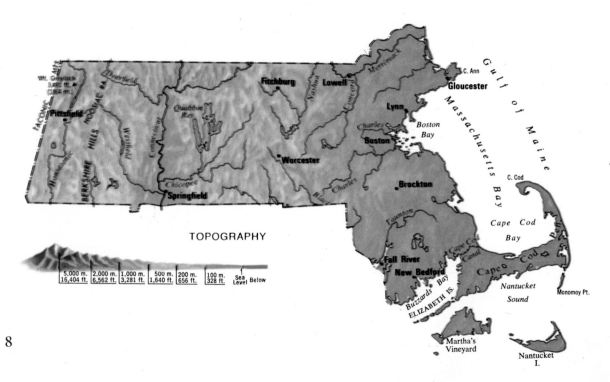

TOPOGRAPHY

5,000 m.	2,000 m.	1,000 m.	500 m.	200 m.	100 m.	Sea	Below
16,404 ft.	6,562 ft.	3,281 ft.	1,640 ft.	656 ft.	328 ft.	Level	

to the south. New York, which is not in New England, is the state to the west. The Atlantic Ocean borders the east and part of the south. Massachusetts is nicknamed the "Bay State." Many of its early settlers lived along the arm of the Atlantic Ocean called Massachusetts Bay.

A cape is a large piece of land that juts out into the water. This is Cape Cod, Massachusetts.

TOPOGRAPHY

Except in the far east, Massachusetts is shaped much like a rectangle. The eastern seacoast is squiggly. Cape Cod sticks out into the ocean like a fishhook. Some offshore islands are also part of Massachusetts. Martha's Vineyard and Nantucket Island are famous islands south of Cape Cod.

Massachusetts' lowest points are in the far east, along the ocean. There, its beaches are at sea level. The state's highest points are in the far west, in the Berkshire Hills and the Taconic Mountains. Mount Greylock, the highest peak in Massachusetts, is in the Taconic Mountains near the state's northwest

Pictured, from left to right: Winter in the Connecticut River Valley, spring in the Berkshire Hills, and fall in the northeastern part of the state

corner. Mount Greylock rises 3,491 feet—two-thirds of a mile—above sea level.

Many rivers flow through little Massachusetts. The Connecticut is the main river. Other rivers include the Taunton, the Charles, the Concord, the Merrimack, the Nashua, the Deerfield, the Westfield, and the Housatonic. Massachusetts is also very wooded. About 60 percent of the Bay State is forested.

Mount Greylock isn't very tall compared to many peaks in the western United States. The nation's highest peak, Alaska's Mount McKinley, is about six times as high as Mount Greylock!

From Ancient Times Until Today

From Ancient Times Until Today

More than one hundred million years ago, dinosaurs lived in Massachusetts. Many dinosaur footprints have been found near the Connecticut River. There were no people yet to hear their thunderous footsteps. The dinosaurs died out long before there were people on earth.

About two million years ago, a cold period began. We call it the Ice Age. Huge blocks of ice called glaciers covered much of North America. In places, the ice was more than a mile thick! All of what is now Massachusetts was under ice. The glaciers dug out deep valleys. Later, these valleys filled with water to become lakes. The glaciers also pushed rock and sand into the ocean to build Cape Cod.

The Ice Age ended about ten thousand years ago. That was about the time when prehistoric Indians first came to what is now Massachusetts. Stone tools and weapons made by the ancient Indians have been found. At first, the Indians hunted, fished, and gathered plants. More than a thousand years ago, they learned to farm.

Opposite: Minuteman statue on Lexington Green

The Indians of Massachusetts

Later, many American Indian tribes lived in Massachusetts. Among them were the Pocomtucs, Pennacooks, Nipmucs, Nausets, Wampanoags, and Massachusetts. Massachusetts was named for the Massachusett Indians.

The Indians helped the first English colonists who arrived in the early 1600s. In fact, the Pilgrims might not have survived without the help of the Indians. But the settlers pushed the Indians off their lands. When the Indians fought back, the settlers killed thousands of them.

Explorers

The Vikings were Norwegians and their neighbors.

We do not know who first explored Massachusetts. Viking Leif Ericson may have reached Massachusetts around A.D. 1000. John Cabot may have reached Massachusetts in 1498 while sailing for England. We do know that in 1602, Englishman Bartholomew Gosnold reached Massachusetts.

The English built their first permanent American town in 1607. It was called Jamestown, Virginia. Captain John Smith, a Jamestown leader, explored New England in 1614. In his book *A*

Description of New England, Smith called Massachusetts a paradise. Captain Smith's book was read by many people in England. Soon some of them decided to move to Massachusetts.

COLONIAL TIMES

In the 1600s, England did not have religious freedom. People who opposed the Church of England could be jailed. Many people decided to move to America, where they could worship in peace. The first large group of people to do this were the Pilgrims. In September 1620, the Pilgrims left England on the *Mayflower.*

The 102 people aboard the *Mayflower* were cold and wet on their 3,000-mile crossing. Many of them felt seasick. Yet mile after mile, day after day, the *Mayflower* continued westward. On November 20, 1620, the Pilgrims reached Cape Cod.

The *Mayflower* anchored near the tip of Cape Cod on November 21. That day, the Pilgrims signed a famous agreement. We call it the Mayflower Compact. The Mayflower Compact created the first self-government in America.

The Pilgrims spent a month looking for the best place to build their first town. In late December,

The Mayflower *was only about 90 feet long–the distance from home plate to first base on a baseball diamond!*

Chief Massasoit

Thanksgiving Day in New England

they chose a spot they called Plymouth. It is said that they stepped on Plymouth Rock while coming ashore. About half the Pilgrims died of disease the first winter. The rest might have died, too, if not for the Indians.

One spring day in 1621, an Indian named Samoset entered Plymouth. "Welcome, Englishmen!" said Samoset, who had learned English from some fishermen. Samoset soon brought his friends Massasoit and Squanto to Plymouth. Massasoit, the chief of the Wampanoags, made a peace treaty with the Pilgrims. Squanto taught them how to grow corn.

Thanks to Squanto, the Pilgrims had a fine harvest in the fall of 1621. The Pilgrims asked Squanto, Massasoit, and about ninety other Indians

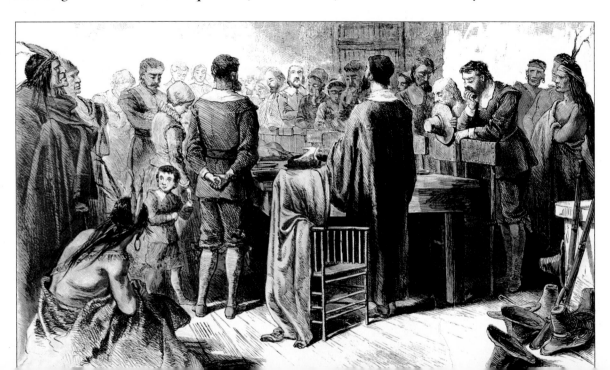

to a feast. That first "Thanksgiving" was the start of the Thanksgiving that is held each November in the United States.

The town of Plymouth was the start of the Plymouth Colony. More shiploads of people arrived. They built more towns. By 1640, the Plymouth Colony had eight towns and twenty-five hundred people.

Meanwhile, a second English colony was being built in Massachusetts. It was called the Massachusetts Bay Colony. This colony had been founded by the Puritans. They were people who belonged to the Church of England but wanted to purify (simplify) it. Salem, the Massachusetts Bay Colony's first town, was founded in 1628. Boston, its main town, was begun in 1630.

Boston in the 1660s

In 1635, the Puritans founded the Boston Latin School, America's first public school. The next year, they founded Harvard College, at Cambridge. It was America's first college. In 1647, the Puritans passed one of the most important laws in American history. It ordered towns of fifty or more families to have a school that was partly paid for by taxes. This marked the start of America's public-school system.

The growth of the two colonies was bad news to the area's Indians. They were being slowly pushed off their lands. King Philip, Massasoit's son, became very angry about this. He decided that his people must drive the settlers out of New England. In 1675 and 1676, he and his warriors fought King Philip's War against the colonists.

King Philip attacked New England towns. The colonists formed armies. The colonial troops killed many Indians. In the end, the Indians could not win against the larger number of settlers. In 1678, the war ended. Several thousand Indians had been killed in King Philip's War. About a thousand New Englanders had also been killed.

Both colonies in Massachusetts grew. But the Massachusetts Bay Colony grew much larger than the Plymouth Colony. England joined the two colonies in 1691. Then there was just one Massachusetts Colony ruled by England. Boston was its capital.

Soon after the two colonies became one, Massachusetts was the scene of a tragic event. Most people believed in witches in the 1600s. Witches were said to make bad weather. It was even thought that they could cause people to die.

During 1692 and 1693, hundreds of people in the Salem, Massachusetts, region called other people witches. It became an easy way to hurt an enemy.

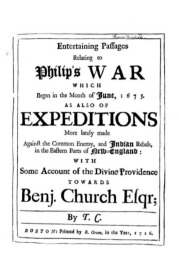

One of the colonists published a story about King Philip's War and other events of the time.

Twenty so-called witches were put to death. This sad event is called the "Salem Witch-Hunt."

During the late 1600s and early 1700s, thousands of new settlers sailed to Massachusetts. Most were English, but some came from Scotland and Ireland. By 1750, Massachusetts had two hundred thousand people and three hundred towns. Boston, with twenty thousand people, was the largest city in the thirteen colonies.

Meanwhile, France was causing trouble for England and its American colonies. France ruled Canada, to the north of England's thirteen colonies. Between 1754 and 1763, England and France fought a war over North America. It is called the

This 1692 witchcraft trial was one of the many that took place in Salem.

French and Indian War. Thousands of Indians helped France. The colonists helped England. Many Massachusetts towns were attacked during this war. England finally won in 1763 and became the main power in North America.

THE REVOLUTIONARY WAR ERA

The long war with France had been costly. By 1764, England was desperate for money. England began taxing the Americans to raise funds. This enraged the colonists.

In 1765, England passed a tax law called the Stamp Act. Americans would have to buy tax stamps and put them on newspapers and other papers. Bostonians protested by wrecking buildings owned by English officials. In 1768, England sent troops

A British tax stamp

The Boston Massacre

to keep order in Boston. On March 5, 1770, English troops killed five Americans in a Boston street fight. Samuel Adams called this the Boston Massacre. Then, on December 16, 1773, the Boston Tea Party took place. Bostonians dumped English tea into the harbor to protest the tax on tea.

American soldiers began to prepare for a possible war with England. Some Massachusetts troops who claimed they could get ready to fight in sixty seconds were called minutemen. They soon had a chance to live up to the name.

On the night of April 18, 1775, English troops marched from Boston toward nearby Lexington. They hoped to capture Samuel Adams and John Hancock. They then planned to seize American war supplies in nearby Concord. The patriots in Boston learned of the redcoats' movements. That night, they told Paul Revere to warn Adams and Hancock. Revere then made his famous midnight ride to the house in Lexington where Adams and Hancock were staying.

Thanks to Revere's warning, Adams and Hancock escaped. Meanwhile, Lexington minutemen gathered on the town green. The British reached Lexington at dawn on April 19, 1775. Moments later, the war began.

Crispus Attucks was one of those killed in the Boston Massacre. He was probably a runaway slave.

The Americas called the English troops redcoats because of their red uniform jackets.

Costumed actors portray the redcoats (left) and the minutemen (right) who took part in the Battle of Lexington.

The British easily won the battle, killing eight Americans and wounding ten. Just one British soldier was wounded. The Battle of Lexington was the first battle of the Revolutionary War (1775-1783). Americans fought this war to free themselves from British rule.

The war's second battle was fought later that same day, at Concord, Massachusetts. Hundreds of American minutemen gathered at Concord. They knew about the American loss at Lexington, and were very angry. The Americans pounded the British at Concord's North Bridge. Then they chased them back to Boston, shooting at them along the way. The Battle of Concord was a great American victory.

An even greater battle was fought in what is now Boston on June 17, 1775. This was the famous

Battle of Bunker Hill. The English claimed victory because they took the hill they wanted. Yet the British lost a thousand men and the Americans lost only four hundred.

During the war, on July 4, 1776, American leaders approved the Declaration of Independence. This paper explained that the thirteen colonies were now the United States. Ever since, July 4 has been celebrated as the nation's birthday.

The war was very difficult for the Americans to win. In fact, it often looked as if the Americans would lose. They refused to give up, though. Nearly ninety thousand Bay Staters served in the Revolutionary War. With their help, the United States finally won its freedom in 1783.

STATEHOOD

In 1787, the new nation made a set of important laws called the United States Constitution. Each of the former thirteen colonies would become a state when it ratified, or approved, the Constitution. Massachusetts approved the Constitution on February 6, 1788, and became the sixth state.

The Bay State produced two of the nation's first presidents. John Adams served as the second president

Citizens viewing the Battle of Bunker Hill

from 1797 to 1801. His son, John Quincy Adams, served as the sixth president from 1825 to 1829.

The Civil War

In 1780, Massachusetts had become the first state to end slavery. Massachusetts people were soon working to end slavery throughout America. David Walker, a black Bostonian, published a book in 1829 calling for the overthrow of slavery. William Lloyd Garrison, a white Massachusetts man, began an antislavery newspaper in 1831. Its name was *The Liberator*. Some Massachusetts people turned their homes into stops on the Underground Railroad. That was a series of hiding places for slaves who escaped north to Canada.

Between 1861 and 1865, northerners and southerners fought the Civil War over slavery and other issues. About 150,000 Massachusetts troops helped the North win the war. Slavery was outlawed in the United States the year the war ended.

Social Issues

Massachusetts people also led the fight for women's rights. In the 1800s, women generally could not

In 1831, William Lloyd Garrison began publishing an antislavery newspaper called The Liberator.

vote or own property. Two Massachusetts-born women, Lucy Stone (1818-1893) and Susan B. Anthony (1820-1906), worked to change this. Their work helped get a law passed in 1920 granting women the vote in the United States. A Massachusetts-born man, Horace Mann (1796-1859), did much to improve the nation's schools. Dorothea Dix (1802-1887), who lived much of her life in Massachusetts, led the fight for better treatment of the mentally ill.

INDUSTRY

Meanwhile, there were changes in how Bay Staters earned their living. Most early Americans had farmed. Manufacturing (making products) became important to the nation in the 1800s.

Lucy Stone was one of the women who led the fight for women's rights.

The Saugus Iron Works made and exported iron in the 1600s, long before the growth of industry in the 1800s.

Textile (cloth) making became very important in Massachusetts. In 1814, Francis Cabot Lowell founded a textile firm near Boston. The company was the first firm that turned raw cotton into cloth under one roof. Lowell was founded as a textile-making center in 1826. It was the nation's first big manufacturing city.

Railroads reached the Bay State in the 1830s. Trains began taking Massachusetts products to many parts of America.

Shoemaking also grew into a major industry. By 1860, Massachusetts led the nation in making shoes and textiles. Almost every Massachusetts town had at least one factory by then. The factories helped Massachusetts attract people from many nations in the 1800s and 1900s.

During World War I (1914-1918) and World War II (1939-1945), the Bay State produced ships.

This shoe factory had its own railroad siding.

It also sent many thousands of people to fight for the country. But there were manufacturing problems in the first half of the 1900s. Other regions made goods more cheaply than Massachusetts could. Also, a period of hardship hit the United States between 1929 and 1939. This period is known as the Great Depression. At times during the depression, less than half of all Massachusetts workers had full-time jobs.

Since about 1950, the Bay State has become a leader in making computers and other "high-tech" (highly technical) items. Many high-tech plants and research labs have been built in the Boston region. They have provided thousands of jobs.

Vannevar Bush, who was born in Everett, helped develop the modern computer in 1930 while he was working at MIT.

RECENT PROBLEMS

Growth in population and industry has had drawbacks. By 1989, Boston Harbor was America's dirtiest harbor. This was partly due to the poisonous chemicals dumped into the harbor by factories. The Housatonic River has also been polluted. By the late 1980s, even the air in some Massachusetts cities was unhealthy to breathe.

The Bay State is working to clean up its water and air. A huge cleanup program is underway in

Boston Harbor. A water-treatment plant should be finished around 1999. The Housatonic River is being cleaned. And in 1990, Massachusetts passed one of the nation's toughest clean-air laws. When it took effect in 1994, it greatly reduced pollution from cars.

Massachusetts also faces money problems. The Bay State has long been known for its fine services. Massachusetts offers better health care than nearly every other state. Bay Staters are among the best-educated Americans. High state taxes have helped create these good services. These taxes rose so high that by 1980 people called the state "Taxachusetts." That year, angry Massachusetts taxpayers voted to lower state taxes. Bay Staters have continued the fight to keep state taxes as low as possible.

A recession is a business slump that is not as serious as a depression.

A recession hit Massachusetts starting around 1990. This added to the state's problems. Many firms went out of business. Thousands of people lost their jobs. By 1993, one in every fifteen Massachusetts workers had no job.

The business slump and the tax revolt have led to a money shortage for the state government. As a result, schools have to get by with fewer teachers. Hospitals are closing. The state faces a great challenge. Massachusetts wants to continue the fine

services for which it is famous. Yet it must find ways to do this that the taxpayers can afford.

Edward Brooke (second from right) was sworn in as a United States senator in 1967.

POLITICAL ACHIEVEMENTS

Several Bay Staters have made political history in recent times. In 1961, Massachusetts Senator John F. Kennedy became the thirty-fifth president of the United States and the first Catholic president. Edward Brooke of Massachusetts was elected to the United States Senate in 1966. He was the first black person to be elected to the Senate in about a hundred years. In 1988, George Bush became the fourth man from Massachusetts to be elected president.

Bay Staters and Their Work

Bay Staters and Their Work

Massachusetts is small. Yet its population of about 6 million is large. As of 1990, Massachusetts had more people than all but twelve other states. The Bay State is home to people of many different backgrounds, including Irish, English, Italian, African, Canadian, Polish, Russian, Chinese, Portuguese, German, Hispanic, French, Cambodian, Haitian, Vietnamese, American Indian, and many others.

Making and selling products is the most popular kind of work in Massachusetts. You may have used many Massachusetts products. They include computers,

Opposite: A Bay State lobster

Computer manufacturing is an important industry in Massachusetts.

Among the products made in the state are jet engines (left) and electronic instruments (right).

television sets, radios, cameras, scientific instruments, books, papers, toys, foods and candy, jet engines, clothes, and shoes. Banking, insurance, and government work are also important, especially in Boston. And the Bay State may have more professors and scientists than any other region of its size on earth. The reason for this is the state's huge number of colleges and research labs.

Farming is less important than it once was in Massachusetts. Yet the state still has several thousand farms. Milk, cranberries, greenhouse flowers, eggs, beef cattle, and hogs are among the main farm goods.

Massachusetts leads the nation in growing cranberries. The Bay State produces about 200 million pounds of cranberries each year. Since there are about 440 cranberries to a pound, that comes to about 90 billion cranberries. Some people string cranberries for their Christmas trees. If all the cranberries Massachusetts grows in a year were strung together, the string would be 700,000 miles long. That's long enough to circle the earth nearly thirty times!

Massachusetts is also a leading fishing state. It is the number-one state for harvesting the tasty shellfish called scallops. Bay State fishermen also bring in cod, lobsters, crabs, clams, shrimp, flounder, and haddock.

Overleaf: Fishing boats in the harbor at Rockport

Fishing (left) and cranberry harvesting (right) are big businesses in Massachusetts.

A Trip Through Massachusetts

A Trip Through Massachusetts

Boston, the state capital and largest city, is a good place to begin a trip through Massachusetts. The Puritans founded Boston in 1630. Today, about half of all Bay Staters live in or around Boston. The city is known as the "Cradle of Liberty," because the rebellion against England began there.

Boston

There is a famous park in downtown Boston called Boston Common. It is the country's oldest park. Cattle used to graze there when the city was young.

An aerial view of Rowe's Wharf, in Boston

Witches were hanged there in the late 1600s. Today, the Common attracts people who want to relax or go for a stroll.

The nearby Massachusetts State House has a golden dome. When the legislators are meeting, visitors can watch them make laws for the Bay State.

Boston's sixty-story John Hancock Tower is New England's highest skyscraper. Yet what makes Boston special are its very old buildings. The city has many landmarks that Paul Revere, Samuel Adams, and John Hancock would know.

The Freedom Trail leads to many of these sites. Bostonians held protest meetings in Faneuil Hall,

Left: Boston's Trinity Church and Hancock Tower
Right: Swan boats moored in the Public Garden pond, across from Boston Common

37

built in 1742. Samuel Adams gave the signal to start the Boston Tea Party at the Old South Meeting House. The Paul Revere House was home to the man who made the famous ride. Not far from Revere's home is the Old North Church. Lamp signals flashing from its steeple told people that the British were heading to Lexington and Concord.

Boston is also noted for its museums. Its Children's Museum is one of the world's great museums for young people. At other Boston museums visitors can learn about such subjects as black history, art, the stars, and dinosaurs. For those who like music, the Boston Symphony Orchestra plays at Symphony Hall. Each summer, the Boston Pops Orchestra plays under the stars.

Three popular pro teams play in Boston: the Celtics of basketball, the Red Sox of baseball, and

Visitors enjoy Boston's Children's Museum (left). Mo Vaughn, of the Red Sox (right), is a star hitter.

the Bruins of hockey. The New England Patriots, a pro football team, play outside Boston in Foxborough. Boston is also the site of the Boston Marathon. It is one of the most famous footraces in the world.

Since Boston is the state capital, thousands of its people work in government. Bostonians also work at such jobs as banking, insurance, fishing, computer making, and book publishing.

Like other big cities, Boston has big problems. There have been harsh feelings between black and white Bostonians in recent years. Many black Bostonians feel blocked from getting good jobs, housing, and schooling. Better race relations are a major Boston goal for the 1990s.

Runners in the 1995 Boston Marathon

GREATER BOSTON

Just west of Boston, across the Charles River, is Cambridge. George Washington took command of the American army in 1775 in Cambridge. Harvard University is in Cambridge. Radcliffe College and the Massachusetts Institute of Technology (MIT) are also there.

Two of the country's most thrilling places are a few miles northwest of Cambridge, at the towns of

Lexington and Concord. At Lexington, you can stand on the spot where the Revolutionary War began. At Concord, you can see where the Americans won their first victory of the war.

CENTRAL MASSACHUSETTS

Don't say WAR-cester, or they'll know you're from out of town. Say WUS-tuhr.

Worcester, the state's second-biggest city, is southwest of Concord. Worcester is home to Holy Cross (founded 1843), New England's oldest Catholic college. The American Antiquarian Society is also in Worcester. Among the library's very old American printed materials are valentines made by Esther Howland (1828-1904). She was a Worcester woman who helped make Valentine's Day a popular holiday.

Springfield, the state's third-largest city, is southwest of Worcester on the Connecticut River. You may have used some of the dictionaries that are published in Springfield. The city is also the home of the Basketball Hall of Fame. Basketball was invented there.

Until about a hundred years ago, there was no popular indoor sport for winter. In 1891, James A. Naismith, a teacher at what is now Springfield College, had an idea. He put up two peach baskets in the gym. His gym class played the world's first basketball game in December 1891.

The Connecticut River Valley, where Springfield is located, has some of the state's richest soil. Potatoes, onions, apples, and tobacco are grown in the valley. Visitors to the Connecticut Valley Historical Museum in Springfield can learn what the river has meant to this area.

WESTERN MASSACHUSETTS

The most mountainous part of Massachusetts starts a few miles west of Springfield. The Berkshire Hills and the Taconic Mountains are in this area.

Springfield, with its Science Museum (left), is located in the Connecticut River Valley (right).

At Hancock Shaker Village near Pittsfield, visitors can see how the Shakers once lived.

Pittsfield, in the Berkshire Hills, is the largest city of far western Massachusetts. Pittsfield's Berkshire County Historical Society has exhibits on pioneer life. It is in the home of Herman Melville, a famous author who lived here in the mid-1800s.

Hancock Shaker Village is near Pittsfield. Ann Lee founded the religious group called the Shakers in 1772 in England. They believed in peace, love, and a simple life. Their name came from their custom of shaking during worship. One of the Shakers' eighteen American towns was the City of Peace, near Pittsfield. At the Hancock Shaker Village, you can see how the Shakers once lived.

Mount Greylock, the highest point in the state, is north of Pittsfield. On a clear day, four states can be seen from the tower on the peak. Three are the nearby states of New York, Vermont, and New Hampshire. The fourth, of course, is Massachusetts.

Plenty of wildlife can be seen in the mountains and woods of western Massachusetts. The state is home to deer, beavers, raccoons, foxes, wild ducks, skunks, and porcupines.

Not far from Mount Greylock, in the town of Adams, is the birthplace of Susan B. Anthony. Also in Adams is the Quaker Meeting House that Anthony and her family attended. The Quakers are a religious group. They were known in early America for their hatred of slavery. Besides her women's-rights work, Susan B. Anthony also fought to end slavery.

Between 1979 and 1981, the United States minted Susan B. Anthony dollars. They were the first United States coins to honor a woman.

Adams is one of hundreds of small towns in Massachusetts. Their village greens and white churches make many of these towns as pretty as a painting.

EASTERN MASSACHUSETTS AND THE COAST

Lowell is in northeastern Massachusetts. It was founded as a textile-making city in 1826. But a hundred years later, Lowell's textile mills were doing poorly. The city seemed to be dying. In recent years, the making of computers has helped breathe new life into Lowell.

East of Lowell, the air begins to taste salty. That is because the Atlantic Ocean is nearby. The famous seaside city of Gloucester is east of Lowell. Gloucester was settled in 1623. It has long been a center for catching and packaging fish. Gloucester's Fishermen's Memorial statue honors all its fishermen who have died at sea.

Gloucester is pronounced GLAWS-tuhr.

Salem is a few miles down the coast from Gloucester. Founded in 1628, Salem was the Massachusetts Bay Colony's first town. Pioneer Village shows what Salem was like in the 1600s. Salem is most famous for its witchcraft trials. The Witch House was the home of one of the judges of the witchcraft trials.

John and Priscilla Alden both came to Massachusetts in 1620 aboard the Mayflower.

The John and Priscilla Alden House is down the coast from Salem, at Duxbury. Built in the 1650s, it is one of only a few houses still standing in which Pilgrims lived.

Plymouth, the Pilgrims' first town, is a short way south of Duxbury. Plimoth Plantation, a large outdoor museum, is a highlight of the town. It has been built to look like the Pilgrims' town of the

1620s. The actors at Plimoth Plantation dress and talk like the Pilgrims.

Fall River, which has long been a big textile-making city, is southwest of Plymouth. New Bedford, a fishing center, is a few miles east of Fall River. In the 1800s, New Bedford was the world's leading port for catching whales. Today, it is against the law to kill whales off the United States coast. But New Bedford fishermen still bring in plenty of scallops, flounder, and cod.

Cape Cod, a short way east of New Bedford, is a good place to end a Massachusetts trip. The cape is a vacation area. People enjoy its beaches and sand dunes. Artists come to Cape Cod to paint seascapes. Boats from Cape Cod take people to the nearby islands of Martha's Vineyard and Nantucket Island.

The Gloucester Fishermen's Memorial (left) honors the fishermen who have died at sea. Plimoth Plantation (right) looks like the Pilgrims' town of the 1620s. The Pilgrims spelled it Plimoth, not Plymouth, as we do.

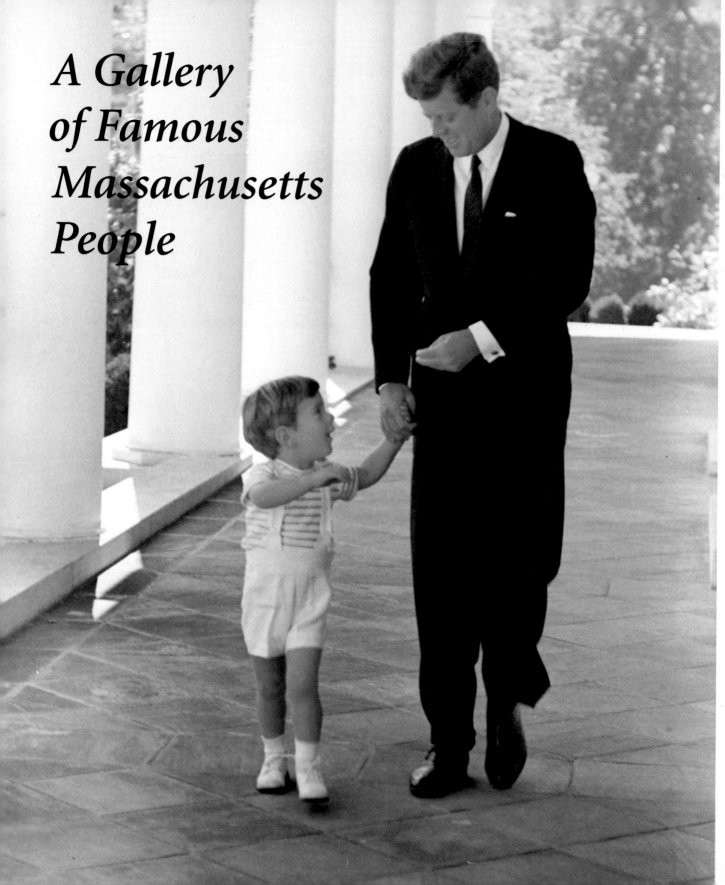

*A Gallery
of Famous
Massachusetts
People*

A Gallery of Famous Massachusetts People

assachusetts has produced more famous people than any other state. More famous people have lived in New York, but many of them were born elsewhere. When it comes to famous early Americans, no state can hold a candle to Massachusetts. A big reason for this is that Massachusetts had the best schools in early America.

Squanto (1585?-1622) belonged to the Patuxet tribe of the Plymouth region. In 1615, an English sea captain kidnapped Squanto and other Indians and took them to Spain as slaves. Squanto escaped. When he returned to his village with another sea captain in 1619, Squanto found that everyone else in his tribe had died of disease. When the Pilgrims arrived in 1620, Squanto was glad for their company. By teaching the Pilgrims to farm, Squanto helped save the Plymouth Colony. Squanto lived with the Pilgrims for the last two years of his life.

Massachusetts was the birthplace of America's most famous political family: the Adams family. **Samuel Adams** (1722-1803) of Boston became known as the "Father of the American Revolution"

Opposite: President John F. Kennedy with his son

John Adams (left) was vice-president under George Washington, the country's first president.

Abigail Adams

*Paul Revere's Ride,
April 19, 1775*

because he did so much to free the country from England. Samuel Adams planned the Boston Tea Party. He also helped organize American leaders in all thirteen colonies.

Samuel's cousins, **John Adams** (1735-1826) and **John Quincy Adams** (1767-1848), were born in Quincy. They were the only father and son who both were president. **Abigail Adams** (1744-1818), who was born in Weymouth, was the only woman who was the wife of one president (John Adams) and the mother of another (John Quincy Adams). She was one of the first American women to speak out for women's rights and against slavery.

Paul Revere (1735-1818) was born in Boston. He became a well-known silversmith. Revere was

one of the tea dumpers at the Boston Tea Party. His most famous deed came in 1775 when he warned Samuel Adams and John Hancock that the British were coming. Some of the many bells Revere made are still rung in New England churches.

John Hancock (1737-1793) was born in Braintree. When Hancock was seven, his father died. He went to live with his rich uncle in Boston. When his uncle died, John Hancock became New England's richest man. He spent a fortune helping the United States win the Revolutionary War. Hancock became the first signer of the Declaration of Independence on July 4, 1776.

John Fitzgerald Kennedy (1917-1963) was born into an Irish-American family in Brookline. During World War II, Kennedy commanded a boat that was cut in half by an enemy ship. He grabbed an injured man's life jacket with his teeth. He swam with the man to an island. In 1960, Kennedy became the youngest person ever elected president. President Kennedy worked for the rights of black people. He also founded the Peace Corps. Sadly, Kennedy was shot and killed in 1963.

The Peace Corps sends Americans to help people in poor countries.

George Bush was born in 1924 in Milton. During World War II, he enlisted in the United States Navy at the age of eighteen. For a while, he

President George Bush with (left to right) his mother, Dorothy Bush, First Lady Barbara Bush holding Millie the dog, and his daughter Doro LeBlond holding her daughter Ellie

was the Navy's youngest airplane pilot. After the war, Bush went into the oil business in Texas. Texans elected him to the U.S. House of Representatives in 1966. Bush served as vice-president for most of the 1980s. He was the forty-first president of the United States from 1989-1993.

Many famous authors have lived in Massachusetts. **Anne Bradstreet** (1613?-1672) was born in England. She sailed to Massachusetts as a teenager in 1630. She became a poet. A book of hers published in 1650 was the first poetry book written in the thirteen colonies.

A more recent Massachusetts author is known as **Dr. Seuss** (1904-1991). His family named him Theodor Seuss Geisel when he was born in Springfield. Using the name Dr. Seuss, he wrote many famous children's books. Among them are *The Cat in the Hat, Green Eggs and Ham,* and *Hop on Pop.*

Other Bay State authors include **Emily Dickinson** (1830-1886), **Amy Lowell** (1874-1925), **Ralph Waldo Emerson** (1803-1882), and **Henry David Thoreau** (1817-1862). Poet **Phillis Wheatley** (1753?-1784) was born in Africa and was kidnapped as a child. She was taken in a slave ship to Boston. There, a couple named Wheatley bought her and named her Phillis. Because Phillis was very bright, the Wheatleys educated her. Phillis began writing poems as a young girl. A book of hers published in 1773 was the first major poetry book by a black American.

The Bay State has produced many inventors. **Eli Whitney** (1765-1825) was born in Westborough. He invented the cotton gin. It helped make the United States the world's leading cotton-producing nation in the 1800s. **Samuel Morse** (1791-1872) was born in what is now Boston. He invented the

This 1956 picture shows Dr. Seuss reading one of his books to a four-year-old girl.

We don't know poet Phillis Wheatley's African name.

Rocky Marciano was born Rocco Marchegiano.

Alexander Graham Bell opened the New York-to-Chicago long-distance telephone line in 1892.

telegraph. It was an early way to communicate quickly over distance. An even better way was invented by **Alexander Graham Bell** (1847-1922), who taught at Boston University. In 1876, Bell invented the telephone. The famous plant breeder **Luther Burbank** (1849-1926) was born in Lancaster.

Massachusetts has also produced some great athletes. One of the best was **Rocky Marciano** (1923-1969), who was born in Brockton. When Marciano was twenty-four, he decided to try pro boxing. He beat one man after another. Finally, he won the heavyweight crown in 1952. Marciano retired in 1956. He had won all forty-nine of his pro bouts, forty-three by knockout!

Leonard Bernstein (1918-1990) had a lighter touch with his hands than Rocky Marciano.

Bernstein was born in Lawrence. When he was nine, a relative sent his family a piano. Leonard sat down and pecked at the keys. Right away he wanted lessons. Bernstein studied music at Harvard University. Later, he became a great conductor and composer. He became famous for writing the musical *West Side Story*.

Clara Barton (1821-1912) was born on a farm near Oxford. She became a nurse. During the Civil War, Barton was called the "Angel of the Battlefield" because she risked her life to nurse the wounded. In 1881, Clara Barton founded the American Red Cross. Each year, the Red Cross helps thousands of disaster victims and soldiers.

Nurse Clara Barton was called the "Angel of the Battlefield."

Home to Clara Barton, Squanto, Susan B. Anthony, many Adamses, John Fitzgerald Kennedy, and the Boston Celtics. . .

The site of Paul Revere's famous ride, of the first Revolutionary War battles, and of Boston's first public school and college . . .

The place where the Pilgrims landed, where Thanksgiving and basketball had their start, and where the telephone and computer were developed.

This is the little state with the big name and the proud history—Massachusetts!

Did You Know?

In 1872, Susan B. Anthony was arrested for voting. She was fined $100 but refused to pay.

Elias Howe, who was born in Spencer, invented the first modern sewing machine in the 1840s.

In 1919, a giant tank broke apart, releasing 2.5 million gallons of molasses in downtown Boston. This Great Boston Molasses Flood killed 21 people and injured 150.

The "Pledge of Allegiance" to the United States flag was written by Boston's Francis Bellamy in 1892.

Bill Russell of the Boston Celtics was pro basketball's Most Valuable Player five times. He coached the Celtics from 1966 to 1969. Russell was the first black head coach of a major American pro sports team.

Boston terriers (the Massachusetts state dog) were first bred in Boston in 1870.

Pencil manufacturing in the United States was begun by William Monroe of Concord in 1812.

Long ago, Boston was home to a professional baseball team called the Boston Beaneaters.

Boston-born astronomer Percival Lowell (brother of poet Amy Lowell) helped discover the planet Pluto.

It is said that the plant called the mayflower (the Massachusetts state flower) was given its name by the Pilgrims.

Make Way for Ducklings, by Robert McCloskey, takes place in Boston. In 1987, a sculpture of Mrs. Mallard and her ducklings was placed in Boston's Public Garden.

No major leaguer has batted as high as .400 since Ted Williams of the Boston Red Sox hit .406 in 1941.

Pilgrim leader William Brewster's sons, Love (for "love of God") and Wrestling (for "wrestling with the Devil") came over with him on the *Mayflower.* Two daughters, Fear and Patience, sailed to Plymouth later.

There is a delicious dessert called Boston cream pie.

In 1897, Boston became the first city in the United States to have a subway train.

MASSACHUSETTS INFORMATION

Area: About 8,300 square miles (only five states are smaller)

Greatest Distance North to South: 110 miles

Greatest Distance East to West: 190 miles

Borders: The states of Vermont and New Hampshire to the north; the Atlantic Ocean to the east; the Atlantic Ocean and the states of Rhode Island and Connecticut to the south; the state of New York to the west

Highest Point: Mount Greylock, 3,491 feet above sea level

Lowest Point: Sea level, along the Atlantic Ocean

Hottest Recorded Temperature: 107° F. (at Chester and New Bedford on August 2, 1975)

Coldest Recorded Temperature: -34° F. (at Birch Hill Dam on January 18, 1957)

Statehood: The sixth state, on February 6, 1788

Origin of Name: Massachusetts was named for the Massachusett Indian tribe; the name is thought to mean "Near the Great Hill"

Capital: Boston

Counties: 14

United States Senators: 2

United States Representatives: 10 (as of 1992)

State Senators: 40

State Representatives: 160

State Song: "All Hail to Massachusetts," by Arthur J. Marsh

State Motto: *Ense petit placidam sub libertate quietem* ("By the sword we seek peace, but peace only under liberty")

Main Nickname: "Bay State"

Other Nicknames: "Old Bay State," "Old Colony State," "Puritan State," "Baked Bean State"

Chickadee

Mayflowers

State Seal: Adopted in 1780; revised version adopted in 1898

State Flag: Adopted in 1908   **State Dog:** Boston terrier

State Flower: Mayflower   **State Fish:** Cod

State Bird: Chickadee   **State Insect:** Ladybug

State Tree: American elm   **State Beverage:** Cranberry juice

State Horse: Morgan horse   **State Colors:** Blue and gold

State Poem: "Blue Hills of Massachusetts," by Katherine E. Mullen

Main River: Connecticut River

Some Other Rivers: Taunton, Charles, Concord, Merrimack, Nashua, Deerfield, Westfield, Housatonic, Blackstone, Chicopee, Millers, Hoosic

Wildlife: Deer, beavers, foxes, porcupines, raccoons, skunks, rabbits, muskrats, pheasants, wild ducks, geese, sea gulls, herons, many other kinds of birds, rattlesnakes and other snakes

Fishing Products: Scallops, cod, lobsters, crabs, clams, shrimp, flounder, haddock, tuna, swordfish, herring

Farm Products: Milk, flowers and other plants grown in greenhouses and nurseries, beef cattle, eggs, hogs, cranberries, potatoes, onions, apples, corn, maple syrup, tobacco

Mining Products: Building stone, sand, gravel, limestone, clay

Manufacturing Products: Computers, computer parts, office machines, airplane engines, many other kinds of machinery and metal products, television sets, radios, medical and scientific instruments, books and other printed materials, many kinds of packaged foods including fish and candy, paper and paper products, sporting equipment and toys, clothing and shoes

Population: 6,016,425, thirteenth among the states (1990 U.S. Census Bureau figures)

Major Cities (1990 state census figures):

Boston	574,283	New Bedford	99,922
Worcester	169,759	Cambridge	95,802
Springfield	156,983	Brockton	92,788
Lowell	103,439	Fall River	92,703

American elm tree

Ladybug

MASSACHUSETTS HISTORY

The Plymouth Rock monument

8000 B.C.–Prehistoric Indians live in the Massachusetts area

A.D. 1500s–American Indians live in the Massachusetts area

1602–Bartholomew Gosnold explores Massachusetts for England

1620–The Pilgrims found Plymouth

1628–The Puritans found Salem

1630–The Puritans found Boston

1635–The Puritans found the Boston Latin School

1636–The Puritans found Harvard, America's first college

1647–The Massachusetts Bay Colony passes a law that is the start of America's public-school system

1675-76–The colonists win "King Philip's War"

1690–The first newspaper in the thirteen colonies is printed in Boston (but lasts just one issue)

1691–The Plymouth and Massachusetts Bay colonies unite to form the Massachusetts Colony, ruled by England

1692–The Salem witchcraft trials take place

1754-63–American colonists help England defeat France in the French and Indian War; to help pay for the war, England soon taxes the Americans

1765–Boston's Sons of Liberty riot against the Stamp Act

1770–In the Boston Massacre, British soldiers kill five Americans

1775–On April 19, the Revolutionary War begins

1776–On July 4, John Hancock of Massachusetts becomes the first person to sign the Declaration of Independence

1783–The United States wins the Revolutionary War

1788–Massachusetts becomes the sixth state

1797–John Adams of Massachusetts becomes the second president of the United States

1800–The population of Massachusetts is 422,845

1825–John Quincy Adams of Massachusetts becomes the sixth president of the United States

1829–David Walker, a free black Bostonian, publishes *Walker's Appeal,* a book that calls for the overthrow of slavery

1831–William Lloyd Garrison starts publishing the antislavery newspaper *The Liberator* in Boston

1861-65–During the Civil War, about 150,000 Massachusetts men help the North win

1891–James A. Naismith invents basketball in Springfield

1900–The population of the Bay State reaches 2,805,346

1912–After textile workers strike at Lawrence, conditions are improved in the country's textile factories

1917-18–After the United States enters World War I, about 198,000 Massachusetts people are in uniform

1920–Women in the United States gain the right to vote

1930–Dr. Vannevar Bush of MIT helps develop the modern computer

1938–A hurricane strikes Massachusetts, killing hundreds

1941-45–After the United States enters World War II, about 556,000 Massachusetts men and women serve

1942–A fire in Boston kills nearly five hundred people

1961–John Fitzgerald Kennedy of Massachusetts becomes the thirty-fifth president of the United States

1971–A program to reorganize state government begins

1988–Happy two-hundredth birthday, Bay State!

1989–Massachusetts-born George Bush becomes the forty-first president of the United States

1990–The population of the Bay State reaches a little more than 6 million

1995–Keith Lockhart becomes the conductor of the Boston Pops Orchestra

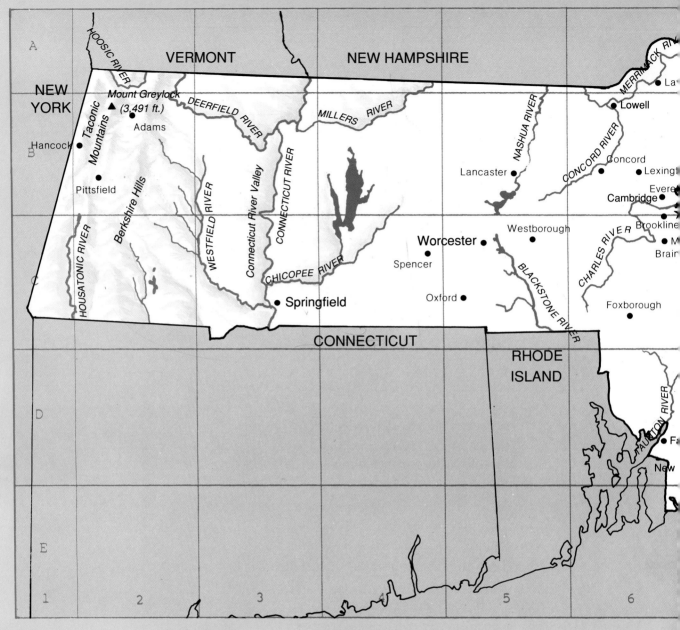

A · VERMONT · NEW HAMPSHIRE

HOOSIC RIVER

NEW YORK

Mount Greylock ▲ (3,491 ft.)

Taconic Mountains

DEERFIELD RIVER

MILLERS RIVER

MERRIMACK RIVER

La

Lowell

NASHUA RIVER

CONCORD RIVER

Concord

Lexing

B · Hancock ·

Adams

CONNECTICUT RIVER

Lancaster ·

Everet

Cambridge ·

Brookline

· Pittsfield

Berkshire Hills

WESTFIELD RIVER

Connecticut River Valley

Worcester ·

Westborough ·

CHARLES RIVER

M

Brair

HOUSATONIC RIVER

CHICOPEE RIVER

Spencer

BLACKSTONE RIVER

C · · Springfield

Oxford ·

Foxborough ·

CONNECTICUT

RHODE ISLAND

D

TAUNTON RIVER

Fa

New

E

1 · 2 · 3 · 4 · 5 · 6

MAP KEY

Adams	B2	Cape Cod Bay	D8	Falmouth	E7	Massachusetts Bay	B7,8
Atlantic Ocean	B,C8,9	Charles River	C6	Foxborough	C6	Merrimack River	A6
Berkshire Hills	B,C2	Chicopee River	C3,4	Gloucester	B7	Millers River	B4
Blackstone River	C5	Concord	B6	Hancock	B2	Milton	C6
Boston	B6	Concord River	B6	Hoosic River	A2	Mount Greylock	B2
Braintree	C7	Connecticut River	B,C3	Housatonic River	C2	Nantucket Island	E8,9
Brockton	C7	Connecticut R. Valley	B,C3	Lancaster	B5	Nashua River	B5
Brookline	C6	Deerfield River	B3	Lawrence	A6	New Bedford	D7
Cambridge	B6	Duxbury	C7	Lexington	B6	Oxford	C5
Cape Cod	C,D8,9	Everett	B6	Lowell	B6	Pittsfield	B2
		Fall River	D6	Martha's Vineyard	E7,8	Plymouth	C7

Quincy	C7
Revere	B7
Salem	B7
Spencer	C4
Springfield	C3
Taconic Mountains	B2
Taunton River	D6
Westborough	C5
Westfield River	B,C3
Weymouth	C7
Worcester	C5

GLOSSARY

antislavery: Against slavery

claimed: Said something as fact

coined: Made up, or invented

communicate: To exchange information

custom: The usual way of doing something; habit

disaster: A sudden event that causes much suffering, such as a flood, an earthquake, a tornado, or a fire

drawback: An unfavorable condition; a disadvantage; a handicap

explores: Travels in unknown lands to seek information

famous: Well known

firm: A company; a business

graze: To feed on growing grass

hardship: Something hard to bear

Hispanic: A person of Spanish-speaking heritage

injured: Hurt; harmed

landmarks: Historic buildings, monuments, or sites

legislators: Persons who make laws

minted: Made money out of metal; coined money

patriot: A person who loves and supports his country

prehistoric: Before written history

protest: A public declaration of objection or dissent

publish: To prepare written material for sale or distribution; issue

rebel: To oppose the authority of a government

rebellion: A fight against one's government; a revolt

revised: Changed; improved; altered

sculpture: Artwork that has been made by carving, chiseling, or molding hard materials

signer: A person who writes his name on a document

subway: A train that runs under the streets of a city; an underground train

telegraph: An electric system of sending messages by wires

thunderous: Making a loud noise that sounds like thunder

tragic: Very sad or terrible

INDEX

Page numbers in boldface type indicate illustrations.

ABOUT THE AUTHOR

Dennis Fradin attended Northwestern University on a partial creative scholarship and graduated in 1967. He has published stories and articles in such places as *Ingenue, The Saturday Evening Post, Scholastic, Chicago, Oui,* and *National Humane Review.* His previous books include the Thirteen Colonies series and the Young People's Stories of Our States series for Childrens Press, and *Bad Luck Tony* for Prentice-Hall. In the True Book series, Dennis has written about astronomy, farming, comets, archaeology, movies, space colonies , the space lab, explorers, and pioneers. He is married and the father of three children.